T0082426

WHAT IF YOU HAD

ANIMAL FEET!?

by **Sandra Markle**

Illustrated by **Howard McWilliam**

Scholastic Inc.

For Mary Mitchell and all the children at West Elementary School in Valley Center, Kansas

A special thank-you to Skip Jeffery for his loving support during the creative process.

Photos ©: cover top and throughout: Dim Dimich/Shutterstock; cover bottom right: Isselee/Dreamstime; cover background: Dave Hughes/Getty Images; back cover top: Angela Waye/Shutterstock; 4: Cubo Images/Robert Harding Picture Library; 4 inset: Ingo Arndt/Minden Pictures; 6: arlindo71/Getty Images; 6 inset: Cheryl Power/Science Source; 8: Nature Picture Library/Alamy Stock Photo; 8 inset: Ingo Arndt/Minden Pictures; 10: Minden Pictures/Superstock, Inc.; 10 inset: BirdImages/Getty Images; 12: Michelle Lalancette/Shutterstock; 12 inset: Bdingman/Dreamstime; 14: NHPA/Superstock, Inc.; 14 inset: D. Parer & E. Parer-Cook/ardea.com/age fotostock; 16: Ardea/Watson, M./Animals Animals; 16 inset: Mike Segar/Reuters; 18: wendy salisbury photography/Getty Images; 18 inset: Lukas Blazek/Dreamstime; 20: Matthew Bowden/Dreamstime; 20 inset: Konrad Wothe/Minden Pictures; 22: kettlewell, Richard/Animals Animals; 22 inset: Chris & Tilde Stuart/Minden Pictures; 24: roberto222/Getty Images; 24 inset: konmesa/Getty Images; 32 top: Chris & Tilde Stuart/Minden Pictures; 32 bottom left: konmesa/Getty Images; 32 bottom right: wendy salisbury photography/Getty Images.

Text copyright © 2024 by Sandra Markle
Illustrations copyright © 2015 by Howard McWilliam

Library of Congress Cataloging-in-Publication Data available

ISBN 978-1-339-01326-8
10 9 8 7 6 5 4 3 2 1   24 25 26 27 28

Printed in the U.S.A. 40
This edition first printing: March 2024

What if one day, you woke up with a wild animal's feet instead of your own?

EASTERN GRAY
KANGAROO

Eastern gray kangaroo hind feet are BIG!
Kangaroos have powerful hind legs.
They can cover 25 feet in one leap
and hop as high as 6 feet!

With eastern gray kangaroo hind feet, you'd easily reach high shelves.

FACT

Sensing danger, a kangaroo thumps its BIG feet to warn others.

HOUSEFLY

Housefly feet have sticky pads.
Walking up walls to stand on the ceiling?
No problem!

With housefly feet, you'd make every basket.

FACT

A housefly has feet with sensors to taste what it steps on.

GREEN BASILISK
LIZARD

A green basilisk (BAS-uh-lisk) lizard's toes
are LONG and fringed.
So, foot slaps trap enough air bubbles
to let it run on water.

With green basilisk lizard feet, no bridges are needed!

FACT

Green basilisk lizard feet are also great swim fins.

CHEETAH

Cheetah feet are paws. Cheetahs can run as fast as 70 miles per hour, which makes them the FASTEST land animal!

With cheetah feet, you'd always catch the bus.

FACT

Like fingerprints, each cheetah paw print is unique.

GRAY WOLF

Gray wolf feet are paws, too.
When running across snow, they spread
WIDE to stop the wolf from sinking.

With gray wolf feet, you'd never need a snow shovel or boots.

FACT

Good blood flow keeps wolf feet toasty—even on ice!

DUCK-BILLED
PLATYPUS

Duck-billed platypus feet are webbed.
That makes the platypus a strong swimmer.
Its sharp toenails let it dig or scratch.

With duck-billed platypus feet, nothing will dare to scare you.

FACT

Male platypus back feet have spurs that inject liquid poison with their kicks.

BARN OWL

Barn owl toenails are talons.
Long, curved, and sharp—they are just
what the owl needs to grip wiggly rats or mice.

With barn owl feet, playtime would be twice as much fun!

FACT

Toothlike edges make a barn owl's middle talons handy combs.

AARDVARK

An aardvark's front toenails are shovel shaped. The aardvark uses these to dig a home plus find yummy ants and termites!

With aardvark feet, you'd easily dig up buried treasure.

FACT

An aardvark flips on its back to fight off enemies with kicks and toenail slashes.

GIANT AFRICAN
MILLIPEDE

A giant African millipede has MANY feet. It needs them all to move dirt when it tunnels underground.

With giant African millipede feet, you'd be the star of every parade.

FACT

If attacked, a millipede curls up to protect its legs and feet.

MOUNTAIN GOAT

Mountain goat feet are hooves.
Each foot has two movable halves.
These let the goat walk and climb safely
in rocky, high places.

With mountain goat feet, you'd be a climbing SUPERHERO.

FACT

A mountain goat's hooves are sharp-edged and have nonslip rubbery pads.

WHITE RHINOCEROS

White rhinoceros (rye-NAH-sur-uhs) feet are stretchy pads with three BIG toes and hooflike nails.

These feet are strong enough to support a 7,000-pound adult white rhino.

With white rhinoceros feet, you could take your family along wherever you go.

FACT

For short dashes, a white rhino can run as fast as 30 miles per hour.

What if you could keep wild animal feet?

Which animal feet would be right for you?

Luckily, you don't have to choose.
Your feet will always be people feet.

They are what you need to walk, run,
dance, skip, hop, or just stand still.

WHAT'S SPECIAL
ABOUT YOUR FEET?

Your feet are built for action
with 26 bones and lots of
muscles to move them.
Your feet bend so easily you
can even dance on your tiptoes!

TO KEEP YOUR
FEET HEALTHY

- Choose shoes that fit properly.
- Wear socks with your shoes.
- Walk, play, and stay active.
- Wash and dry your feet daily.

OTHER BOOKS IN THE SERIES